Robin Hood

Titles in the series

The Magic Key

Robin Hood

Story by Roderick Hunt

Illustrations by Alex Brychta

OXFORD

UNIVERSITY PRESS

Biff and Wilma went to the pantomime.

They went with Wilma's mum.

They had a friend called Anneena.

Anneena went to the pantomime with them.

The pantomime was about Robin Hood.
Robin Hood was a good man.
He lived in a wood with his men.
Everyone liked Robin Hood and they gave
a cheer every time he came in.

There was a bad man called the Sheriff.

Nobody liked the Sheriff.

He wanted to catch Robin Hood and
lock him up.

'Look out, Robin!' shouted the children.

The next day, Wilma and Anneena went
to play with Biff.
They sang a song about Robin Hood.
Wilma played her guitar and Anneena
played her recorder.

Kipper didn't like the song.

He put his hands over his ears and made a face.

'Woooooooh,' said Kipper.

Kipper had a key round his neck.

It was the magic key.

Biff was cross with Kipper.

'Put the key back in the box,' she said.

Suddenly the key began to glow.

'Look out, Anneena,' said Biff. 'This is
a magic key and the magic is working.
It's time for an adventure.'

The magic took the children to a wood.
It was the wood where Robin Hood lived.
The children could see Robin with some
of his men.

Robin Hood had not seen the children.

Anneena was frightened.

'I hope he is a good man,' she said.

'Come on,' said Kipper, 'I can smell food.'

Robin Hood saw the children.

'Who are you?' he asked.

'Are you lost in the woods?
Come and sit down.'

The children sat by the fire.

'We saw you in a play,' said Anneena. 'We can sing a song about you.'

'Oh no!' said Kipper. 'Not the song again.'

Biff, Wilma, and Anneena sang the song.
The song said everyone liked Robin but
nobody liked the Sheriff.
Robin Hood's men gave a cheer.

'What a good song!' said Robin Hood.

'Sing it to me again.'

Kipper looked inside a big black pot.

Nobody saw the Sheriff coming.

Suddenly the Sheriff's men ran in.
They grabbed Robin Hood and put a
rope round him.
'Got you at last!' said the Sheriff.

They jumped on Robin's men and they
grabbed Biff, Wilma, and Anneena.
They put them all into a cart.
'Take them away!' said the Sheriff.

Kipper hid in the big black pot.

The Sheriff's men didn't see him.

'Oh no!' he said. 'What can I do?

I must help them.'

The Sheriff took them to a village.

He said, 'My castle is too far away, so we
will stop here.

One of my men will see you don't get away.'

Kipper went up to the man.

He gave the man a sweet.

'What is that thing?' he asked.

'You lock people up in it,' said the man.

'You can't lock people in that,' said Kipper. 'You can't get them in.'

'Oh yes you can,' said the man. 'Look.'

He put in his head and his hands.

'Ha!' said Kipper. 'You fell for it.'

He locked the man in and took away his keys.

'Grrr!' said the man.

Kipper set them free.

'Come on, everyone,' said Robin Hood.

'Let's go back to the woods.

We don't want the Sheriff to catch us.'

They went to a new part of the woods.

'Three cheers for Kipper,' said Robin Hood.

'Now let's sing that song about me again.'

'Oh no!' said Kipper.

Suddenly the magic key began to glow.

'Just in time,' said Kipper.

'It's time for us to go.'

'Goodbye,' said the children.

'Goodbye,' said Robin Hood, 'and thanks.'

'What an adventure!' said Anneena.

'I liked Robin Hood and his men.

Let's sing the song.'

'Aaaaaah!' said Kipper.

Questions about the story

- How did the children learn about Robin Hood?
- Who was Robin Hood, and when did he live?
- Who was the Sheriff, and why did nobody like him?
- How many merry men can you see with Robin Hood?
- Why did Kipper hide in the big black pot?
- How did Kipper trick the man?
- Who kept singing the song?
- What did Kipper bring back from this adventure?

UNIVERSITY PRESS

Great Clarendon Street, Oxford OX2 6DP

Oxford University Press is a department of the University of Oxford.
It furthers the University's objective of excellence in research, scholarship,
and education by publishing worldwide in

Oxford New York

Athens Auckland Bangkok Bogotá Buenos Aires Calcutta Cape Town
Chennai Dar es Salaam Delhi Florence Hong Kong Istanbul Karachi
Kuala Lumpur Madrid Melbourne Mexico City Mumbai Nairobi
Paris São Paulo Shanghai Singapore Taipei Tokyo Toronto Warsaw

with associated companies in Berlin Ibadan

Oxford is a registered trade mark of Oxford University Press
in the UK and in certain other countries

British Library Cataloguing in Publication Data

Data available

ISBN 0 19 919425 4

Printed in Hong Kong